With best wishes to
Jean & Brian
(See P. 52)

WHO LIVES IN A TREE?

By the same author:

Monthly Poetry Prompts Page, Child Education, Scholastic, 1994 – 1995

Fly Eagle Fly, Picture Ladybird, 1996

Contributor to *Teachers' Resource Books,* Ginn, 1996

Contributor to *The Theme Books and Wishing Well Series,* Scholastic, 1996 – 2001

Contributor to *A Big Book of Rhymes,* Collins, 2005

WHO LIVES IN A TREE?

Jan Pollard

Illustrated by Jan and Nigel Pollard

Book Guild Publishing
Sussex, England

First published in Great Britain in 2006 by
The Book Guild Ltd
25 High Street
Lewes, East Sussex
BN7 2LU

Copyright © Jan Pollard 2006

The right of Jan Pollard to be identified as the author of
this work has been asserted by her in accordance with the
Copyright, Designs and Patents Act 1988.

All rights reserved. No part of this publication may be reproduced, transmitted, or stored in a retrieval system, in any form or by any means, without permission in writing from the publisher, nor be otherwise circulated in any form of binding or cover other than that in which it is published and without a similar condition being imposed on the subsequent purchaser.

All characters in this publication are fictitious and any resemblance to real people, alive or dead, is purely coincidental.

Typesetting in Times by
MRM Graphics Ltd

Printed and bound in Singapore under the supervision of
MRM Graphics Ltd, Winslow, Buckinghamshire

A catalogue record for this book is available from
The British Library

ISBN 1 84624 039 5

*For Joshua
With Love*

CONTENTS

Foreword ix

4–5 years

Bath Water	1
The Picnic Table	2
Autumn Colours	3
Teddy at the Doctor's	4
Finger Rhyme	5
Odd Socks	6
Little Spider	7
The Baker	8
The MOQ Cat	9
At the Seaside	10
The Garden	11
Playing Doctors and Nurses	12
What Would You Like To Be?	13
The Seashore	14
The Barbeque	15
Can You Find the Tiger?	16
Travelling	17
Ready for Anything	18
Colour Magic	19
The Puppet	20
The Busy Farmer	21
Guinea Pigs	22
Painting	23
The Outing	24
The Robot	26
The Wooden House	27
Hair	28
Black Cat	29
Wake Up	30
The Tree	31
Birthdays	32
Getting Somewhere	33
Going Places	34

6–7 years

Growing Up	35
Happy Easter	36
Growing Seeds	37
The Mouse	38
Colours of Fruit	39
The Rocking Horse	40
Harvest	41
Floating by	42
Who Lives in the Sea?	43
Narrow Boats	44
Slow Snail	45
Muddle	46
The Worm	47
Windy Nights	48
Shadows	49
Gran's Glasses	50
Snow	51
The Witch of the South	52
Air	53
Our Bones	54
Leaves	55
Tickle me Pink	56
Castles in the Air	57
The Dinosaur	58
Swim Dolphin, Swim	59
The Halloween Feast	60
Chinese Dragon Dance	61
The Frog	62
The Fossil	63
The Green Man	64
A Long Time Ago	66
Amelia, Cordelia, Lucinda Blott	67
Gulp!	68

FOREWORD

I first worked with Jan Pollard some years ago when I was commissioning resources for *Themes for Early Years* and *Early Years Wishing Well* books for nursery and reception teachers, published by Scholastic. Jan always managed to come up with just the right material, which wasn't surprising since she has had a great deal of experience both teaching and writing for young children.

Writing good poetry for a young audience is far from easy. Children cannot be fobbed off with badly metered, rhyming doggerel – a mistake made by many an aspiring children's poet. Jan, however, has the skill to pick appropriate, interesting subjects and give them an easy metre and rhyme which children find fun. *Fly, Eagle, Fly!* (published by Ladybird) demonstrated that her poetry can also stand alone as a beautifully illustrated picture book.

In this eclectic collection can be found seasons, celebrations, domestic mundanities, and every aspect of a child's world and day-to-day life. It's a panorama of colour and rhyme which I know will bring pleasure to every reader, young or old, and provide a wealth of resources for teachers.

Jackie Andrews

Jackie Andrews has worked in children's publishing for many years, writing, editing and reviewing. She is now a consultant editor and writer for a children's publisher and has launched a series of fantasy novels for teenagers, published by Simon & Schuster.

Bath Water

The water rises in my bath,
When I get in to wash.
Good job I'm not an elephant,
It would be an awful

SPLOSH!!

The Picnic Table

Daisies for our dinner,
Buttercups for tea.
I've spread them on the table,
So you can dine with me.

What a lovely picnic,
But it's really such a lot,
I think it would be better,
If we put them in a pot.

Autumn Colours

Autumn is golden,
Golden and brown.
Look at the leaves
As they tumble down.

Put them under paper
And crayon on the top.
Cut out your own leaves.
Have you made a lot?

Teddy at the Doctor's

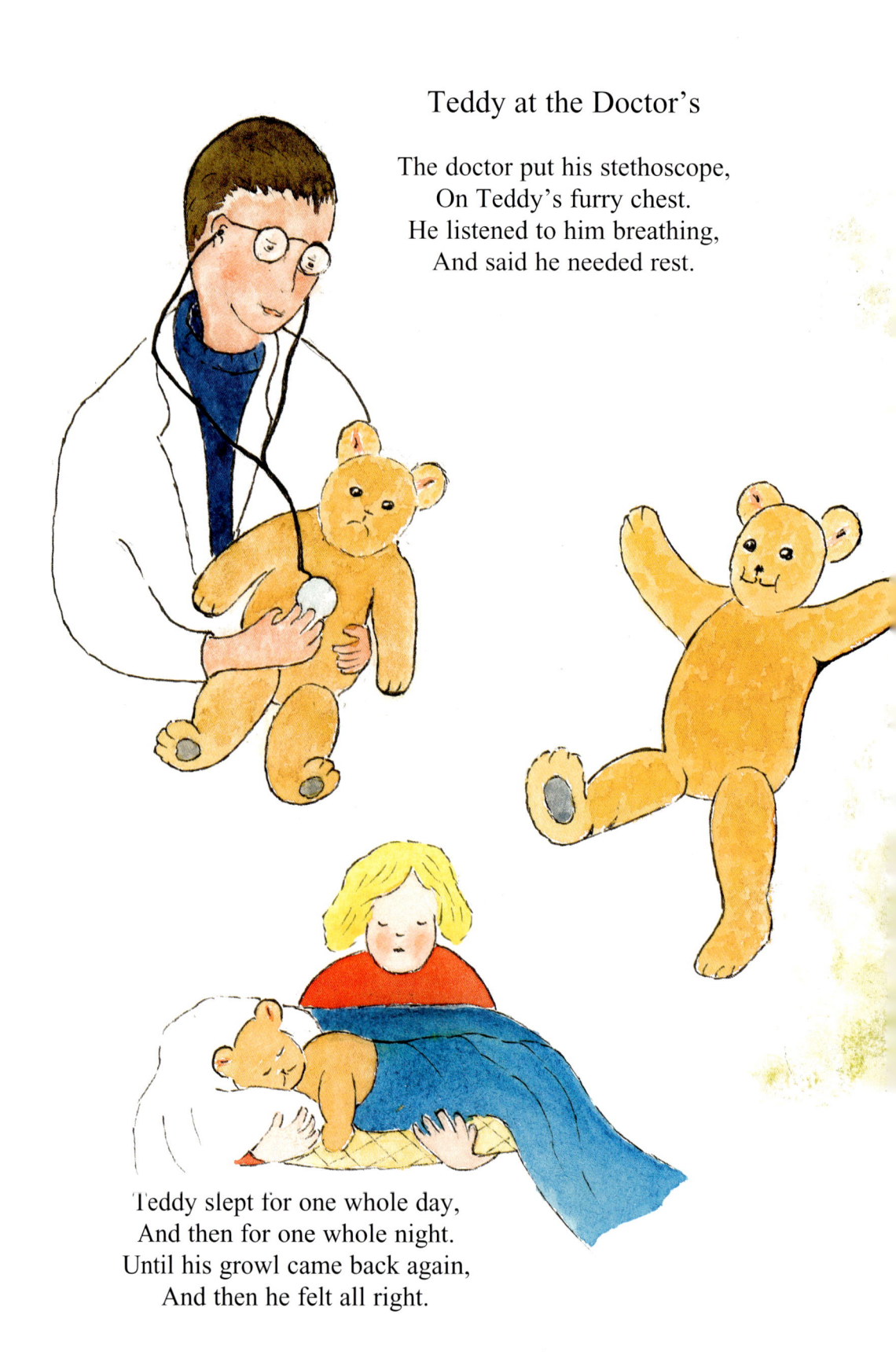

The doctor put his stethoscope,
On Teddy's furry chest.
He listened to him breathing,
And said he needed rest.

Teddy slept for one whole day,
And then for one whole night.
Until his growl came back again,
And then he felt all right.

Finger Rhyme

One leaf growing on the tree,
As pretty a leaf as you could see.

Then another leaf uncurled,
tretching out to see the world.

A third leaf came to join the others,
Happy to find he had some brothers.

A fourth leaf thought he'd come to see
If he liked living on the tree.

And then the fifth leaf raised his head,
Emerging from his wintry bed.

1, 2, 3, 4, 5, you see.
Little green leaves, on the old oak tree.

Odd Socks

Sometimes I wear a blue sock,
On the other foot, one red.
It's only because I'm lazy,
When I get out of bed.

As two of each colour make a pair,
Why is it when I look for them
They never seem to be there?

Little Spider

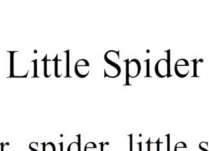

Spider, spider, little spider,
hanging from a thread.
I can see you as I'm lying
snugly in my bed.
Spider, spider, little spider,
don't come down I beg.
I really couldn't bear it
if you landed on my head.

The Baker

Baker, baker, mix the dough,
Add the yeast and watch it grow.
In the oven it must pop,
Take it out when piping hot.

Can you smell it?
Here it comes.
Hot new bread, and
currant buns.

The MOQ Cat

The M makes his ears,
His face is round and fat.
Draw them on the Q
And you have made a cat.

Two dots for his eyes,
And a smile in place,
And lots and lots of whiskers
To make a happy face.

At the Seaside

I splash in the water,
And jump in the sea,
And run up the beach,
When its time for tea.

I build a castle
With my bucket and my spade,
And watch it wash away
In the next big wave.

Who loves the sunshine?
Who loves the sea?
Who loves the seaside?
Me! Me! Me!

The Garden

It's quiet in the garden,
And you can't hear a sound,
Yet all the little seeds,
Are growing in the ground.

When it gets warmer,
And the rain begins to fall,
They send down their roots,
And begin to grow tall.

Up come the flowers,
All in a row.
Pushing through the earth,
From their bed, down below.

Lots of little daisies,
Growing in the grass.
Nodding their heads at us,
As we walk past.

Playing Doctors and Nurses

Has your doll got a cold, nurse?
Please blow her nose.
Are her feet hot, nurse?
Just feel her toes.

Has she got spots, nurse?
I'll look at her chest.
I think your doll's got measles
And needs some rest.

Doctors and nurses
Is our favourite game.
Every time we play it
It's never the same.

What Would You Like To Be?

Would you like to be an elephant,
And sway from side to side?
With a howdah on your back,
Taking people for a ride.

Would you like to be a camel,
With a great big hump?
And plod through the desert,
Lumpity, lumpity, lump.

Would you like to be a monkey,
Climbing up a tree?
And when you reach the very top,
Throw down fruit to me.

Would you like to be a tiger,
Going for a prowl?
And if you meet another one,
Begin to snarl and growl.

Would you like to be a bear,
Fishing in the river?
Catching salmon in your paws,
To eat for your dinner.

Would you like to be a kangaroo,
Going for a hop?
Leaping through the gum trees,
Until you want to stop.

The Seashore

The tide comes in and the tide goes out,
Once every day and once every night.

Crashing over rocks
And running up the strand,
And when we go to look for shells
We leave footprints in the sand.

The Barbecue

Here is our barbecue,
sizzling hot.
Let's have a look, to see
what we've got.

Pieces of chicken, burgers too.
Lots and lots of sausages,
Sausages, sausages,
I love sausages.
How about you?

Can You Find the Tiger?

Tiger, tiger, orange and black,
With lots of lines across his back.
In the forest, dark and green,
The stripey tiger can't be seen.

Travelling

How far to school?
Not far by car.
How far to the sea?
Not far for me.
How far home again?
Not far by train.

How far to Spain?
Not far by plane.
How far to the shop?
Not far if you hop.
How far from here?
To where, my dear?

Ready for Anything

Lace up your shoes,
Pull on your socks,
Put your sandwiches
Into a box.

Put on your anorak,
Pull on your hat,
Hands in your gloves,
And your bag on your back.

You're ready now,
For the rain or the snow,
You'll keep really warm,
Wherever you go.

Colour Magic

Red and blue make purple,
Yellow and blue make green,
Red and yellow make orange,
The loveliest colours you've seen.

Paint them on your paper,
Fold it and press it flat,
It makes a beautiful butterfly,
Now what do you think of that!

The Puppet

Here is a puppet
on a string,
You can make him do
just anything.
Lift up his hand
to scratch his nose,
Bend him over
to touch his toes.
One foot up
and one foot down,
Here he goes,
walking into town.

If you were a puppet
on a string,
Someone could make you
do anything.

The Busy Farmer

Farmer, farmer,
milk the cow,
Cream and butter,
we'll have now.

Farmer, farmer, feed
the pig,
Oink, oink, oink,
he's getting big.

Farmer, farmer,
shear the sheep,
Nice warm clothes
for us to keep.

Farmer, farmer, cut
the wheat,
Made into bread,
it's good to eat.

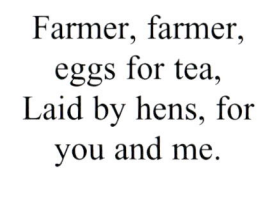

Farmer, farmer,
eggs for tea,
Laid by hens, for
you and me.

Guinea Pigs

Two little guinea pigs
Black and white and friendly,
Lived in our garden shed
And had a little family.
Four little guinea pigs
Grew and grew and grew,
And soon they were just as big
As the very first two.

Six little guinea pigs,
Some black, some white, some brown,
Had eight little babies,
So we took them all to town.
We took them to the pet shop
And hoped they'd buy them, when
On taking them out of the cardboard box,
We found that there were TEN!

Painting

I paint a little, smudge a lot,
Drop my paints, and make a spot.
Spill the water on my train,
Wipe it up and start again.
Sit me down upon a chair,
Find I've paint stuck in my hair.
Look who's painting, it's the cat!
Get down, puss, you can't do that.
There are paint marks everywhere.
On my painting, on the chair,
On my shirt, but I don't care.
I've got lots of shirts to spare.

I want to go outside and play,
So why did it have to rain today!

The Outing

Walking, talking, pointing, watching.
Running, chasing, skipping, jumping.

Sitting, eating, munching, drinking.

Climbing, falling, tumbling, bumping.
Hurting, crying, wiping, drying.
Bathing, washing, splashing, playing.

Reading, listening,
Sleeping, dreaming.

The Robot

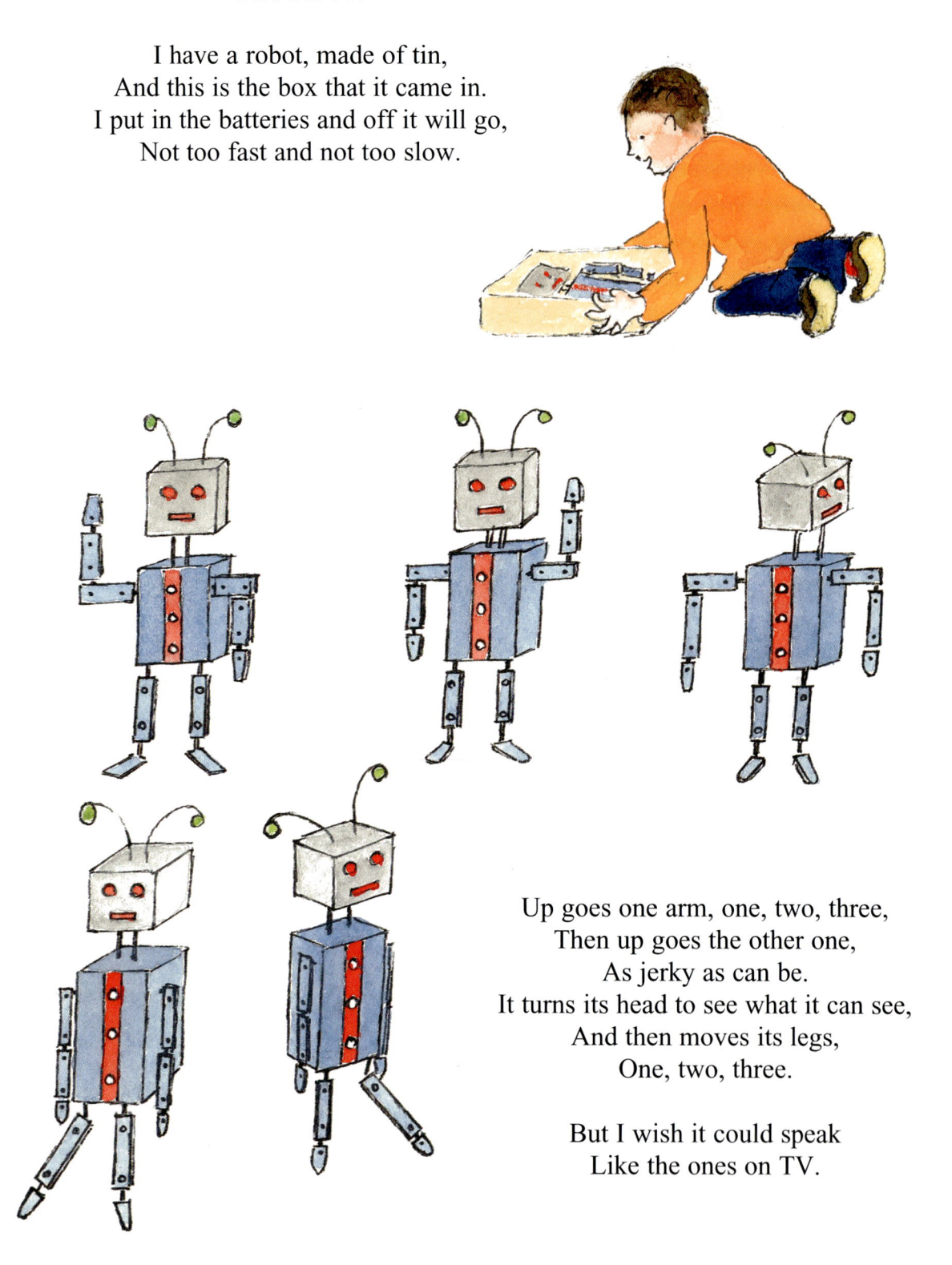

I have a robot, made of tin,
And this is the box that it came in.
I put in the batteries and off it will go,
Not too fast and not too slow.

Up goes one arm, one, two, three,
Then up goes the other one,
As jerky as can be.
It turns its head to see what it can see,
And then moves its legs,
One, two, three.

But I wish it could speak
Like the ones on TV.

The Wooden House

In the wooden playhouse,
There are lots of wooden things.
A wooden chair and table,
And puppets on their strings.

There's a dolls' house in the corner,
And a rocking horse to ride,
And a big wooden cupboard,
To put the toys inside.

Coloured pencils, paper, books,
And blocks to build a tower.
In the wooden playhouse,
We could spend a happy hour.

Hair

Fair hair, red hair,
Brown hair, black hair.
What does it matter
About the rest?

I love my hair,
Black and curly,
Plaited in patterns,
Mine's the best!
Tied in bunches,
With ribbons of red,
Or threaded with beads,
Around my head.

Black Cat

Black cat, what are you at?
Where are you going, and why?
Why are your whiskers twitching like that?
Why does your fur lie flat on your back?
Why are you waving your tail in the air?
Why are your eyes open wide in a stare?
What are you watching there by the tree?
Is it a bird or a leaf you can see?
Black cat, just what are you at?

Wake Up

Wake up prickly hedgehogs,
With your beady little eyes.
Spring has come again,
To give you a surprise.

Wake up little dormice,
The winter's gone away.
Uncurl yourselves and have a stretch,
The sun is out today.

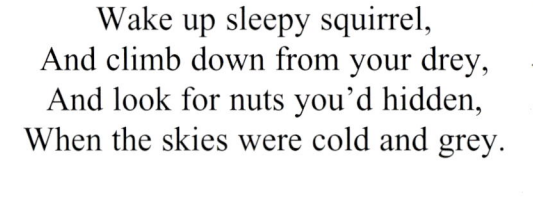

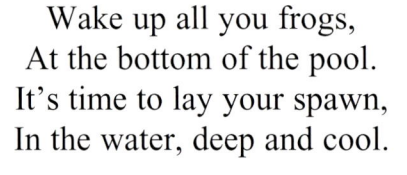

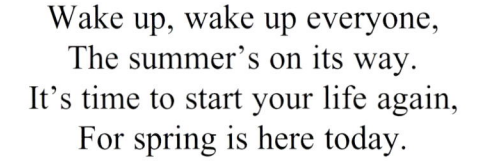

Wake up sleepy squirrel,
And climb down from your drey,
And look for nuts you'd hidden,
When the skies were cold and grey.

Wake up all you frogs,
At the bottom of the pool.
It's time to lay your spawn,
In the water, deep and cool.

Wake up, wake up everyone,
The summer's on its way.
It's time to start your life again,
For spring is here today.

The Tree

Who lives in a tree?
I do, says the bee.
I buzz around
With my nest near
the ground.

I do, says the bird.
Haven't you heard
me sing to my mate,
as our nest we make?

I do, says the fly
As he goes by.

I do, says the beetle.
I bore into the bark,
and lay tiny grubs,
deep down in the dark.

I do, says the squirrel.
I build a drey,
So my babies can keep
safe, warm and dry.

I do, says the moth.
I sleep through the day,
but when the night comes,
then I fly away.

Who lives in a tree?
I wish it was me.

Birthdays

Every year another candle
Added to your birthday cake.
How old are you now I wonder?
How many birthdays does that make?
Getting bigger, growing taller,
Larger shoes to fit your feet,
Every year we all grow older,
Birthdays are a special treat.
Fun and games and happy faces,
With lots of presents from our friends.
Every year we all have birthdays,
Let's hope birthdays never end.

Getting Somewhere

How shall we get there?
It isn't very far.
Shall we walk together
And not go by car?

How shall we get there?
It's a long way away.
Shall we travel on a bus
And have a nice day?

How shall we get there?
Shall we take a boat?
When the wind fills the sails
It will keep us afloat.

How shall we get there?
Shall we go by train?
And when we've all got there
We'll go back home again.

Going Places

A jumbo is an elephant.
It also is a plane.
They both take people far away
And bring them back again.

A joey is a kangaroo,
Inside a furry pouch.
His mother leaps about with him.
OUCH! OUCH! OUCH!

Cygnets are baby swans,
And swim by mother's side.
Sometimes they climb on to her back,
And she gives them a ride.

Mum's car is called a Beetle.
The inside seats are black.
She drives us everywhere in it,
And we sit in the back.

Growing Up

When I was born I was very small,
I couldn't sit up, or walk, or crawl.
I hadn't any teeth so I couldn't eat,
And fed from a bottle, through a teat.

As I grew older I used a spoon,
And walked unsteadily round the room.
Teeth grew in my gums so I could eat,
Puddings and fish and minced-up meat.

Once I could run, my legs grew stronger,
My body grew taller and my arms got longer.
Under my baby teeth my big teeth grew,
And as they fell out my others came through.

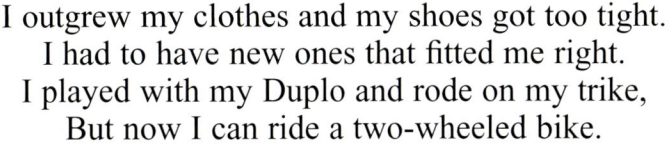

I outgrew my clothes and my shoes got too tight.
I had to have new ones that fitted me right.
I played with my Duplo and rode on my trike,
But now I can ride a two-wheeled bike.

I can eat my meals with a knife and a fork,
I can read and write and I talk and talk and talk.
I have my hair cut without any fuss,
And help carry shopping when we go on the bus.

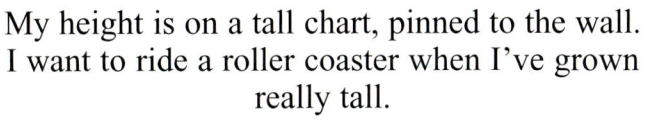

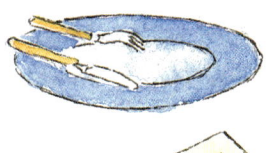

My height is on a tall chart, pinned to the wall.
I want to ride a roller coaster when I've grown really tall.

Happy Easter

Red is the colour of Christmas,
And green is the colour of spring,
But Easter is a yellow time,
Yellow in lots of things.

Yellow in the fluffy chicks,
With spindly little legs.
Yellow in the ribbons,
Which tie our Easter eggs.

Yellow in the daffodils,
Swaying to and fro,
Yellow crocuses and tulips,
Which in our garden grow.

Yellow in my breakfast egg,
And custard on my pie.
Yellow on the simnel cake,
And sunshine in the sky.

Growing Seeds

Springtime comes and bees are buzzing,
Round the flowers and round the trees.
Spreading out the yellow pollen,
So the plants can make their seeds.

Pips from apples, pears and melons,
Tomatoes, marrows, all of these,
Stones from plums and nectarines,
They grow into plants and trees.

Sunshine makes the fir cones open,
Spreading out their flat brown seeds.
When it's cold and snowy weather,
They've grown into Christmas trees.

Inside a cover, green and spiky,
Lies a treasure, snug inside.
Big and shiny, snooth and glossy,
Chestnut conkers, safely hide.

From small acorns, oak trees grow,
Plant them and you'll find it so.
Peas and beans and pips will sprout,
It's fun to do, so try it out.

The Mouse

The mouse in our house,
Runs over the floor and past the door,

Finds the cheese and ham and peas,
Upsets tins and eats from bins,
Spills peas on the ground,
And rolls them around,
Has flour on his nose and on his toes.

When we have a cat he won't like that,
She'll creep about and smell him out.
So get out of our house,
You naughty mouse.

Colours of Fruit

6 bananas in a bunch.
A yellow banana for my lunch.

5 round apples from the tree.
A rosy red apple, just for me.

4 green pears, speckled with brown.
Not ripe yet, so I'll put them down.

3 round oranges, Oh! Oh! Oh!
Squeeze them, drink them, there you go.

2 pink peaches, fat and sweet,
Soft and furry and ready to eat.

I can see one purple plum.
Would you like it?
Yum! Yum! Yum!

The Rocking Horse

My horse has a bridle and saddle of red,
And stands in my room at the foot of my bed.
I sit on his back and take hold of his reins,
Ready to gallop through streets and through lanes.

Galloping, galloping, faster and faster,
He is my horse and I am his master.
We leap up and we leap down,
Through the trees and into town.
Over the cobblestones, clip, clop, clip,
Walking with care so he doesn't slip.

Into the countryside, over the lea,
My horse goes galloping, fancy free.
Backwards and forwards, faster and faster,
He is my horse and I am his master.

Harvest

H is for harvest,
from flour we make bread.
A is for apples,
all rosy and red.
R is for runners,
the beans that grow tall.
V is for vegetables,
we eat them all.
E is for eggs,
some big and some small.
S is for sunshine,
to ripen the wheat.
T for thanksgiving,
for the food that we eat.

Floating By

A lady who fell off a boat,
Found her skirt would keep her afloat.
When she came to the edge,
She stood on a ledge.
Grabbed hold of a trolley,
Put up her brolly.
And went shopping,
In town – for some veg!

Who Lives in the Sea?

I do, says the fish,
I swim where I wish.
But I hide in the dark,
Well away from the shark.

I do, says the whale,
As he lifts his big tail.
While I cruise along,
I sing a whale song.

I do, says the seal,
I eat fish for my meal.
Like the penguins I see,
As they swim around me.

I do, says the crab,
With my big front claws,
I push all my food,
In through my jaws.

I do, says the jellyfish,
But don't come near me.
My tentacles sting,
If you swim in the sea.

I do, says the octopus,
As his arms wave around.
I squirt ink on my enemies,
And they soon go to ground.

Who lives in the sea?
I'm glad it's not me.

Narrow Boats

Narrow boats, coloured boats,
Cruising along the river,
Painted with diamonds,
Of yellow, red and green.
If we lived on a narrow boat,
Chugging along the river,
You'd feel like a king,
And I'd feel like a queen.

Slow Snail

Slow snail, slithering silently,
How long it takes to slide down the path.
Slow snail, slithering silently,
Watch out for that bird there, taking a bath.

Slow snail, slithering silently,
Why do you leave such a long silver trail?
Slow snail, slithering silently,
That bird has seen you, poor little snail.

Slow snail, slithering silently,
Pull in your eyes and curl inside tight.
Slow snail, slithering silently,
Stay very still and you'll be all right.

Muddle

There are things in the cupboard,
And things on the floor,
And things in the kitchen,
Piled up behind the door.

There are dolls on the chairs,
With their clothes on the ground.
Puzzles, Lego, trains and cars,
Are scattered all around.

There are paints on the table,
And crayons by my feet,
And when its time to have our tea,
There isn't room to eat.

We can never find our things,
Because of all the muddle.
If we were all more tidy,
It would save a lot of trouble.

The Worm

Wriggling, squirming, slowly turning,
The worm slides into his earthy hole.
Moving his segments from tail to head,
He pulls leaves down to his underground bed.

Wriggling, squirming, slowly turning,
The worm slithers up towards the light.
Leaving a cast on the dew-laden grasses,
Not knowing whether it's day or night.

Wriggling, squirming, slowly turning,
The worm sifts the soil and lets in the air.
Turning it over to make the ground richer
Working so hard in his secret lair.

Wriggling, squirming, slowly turning,
The worm is caught by a prodding beak.
An early bird who is looking for breakfast,
Finds the worm a tasty treat.

Windy Nights

I snuggle right down,
And cuddle up tight,
While the wind and the rain,
Rush around all the night.
I lie on soft pillows,
Covered up to my head.
I'm glad I'm not outside,
But inside, in bed.

Where have the birds gone,
The moths and the bees?
Where can they hide
On nights such as these?
When morning has broken,
I wake in the light,
To hear the birds singing,
And bees in full flight.

Shadows

What is that thing across the floor?

Now it's moving up the door.

Sometimes I see it on the wall,
Getting longer, growing tall.

Whenever I move it moves with me.
I wonder why? What can it be?

Gran's Glasses

Gran knitted me a jumper,
It was red and white and blue.
And on the front she knitted,
A funny cockatoo.
She didn't get the pattern right,
As everyone can see,
For the bird looks like a frying pan,
Up in a rhubarb tree.

Gran knitted me a sweater,
It was yellow, green and black.
And on the front she knitted,
What looked like an old sack.
She *said* it was a monkey,
In a green and leafy tree,
But I think she needs new glasses,
Or else it must be me!

Snow

Snow,
　　Snow,
　　　　Snow,
　　　　　　Snow,
Falling softly, falling gently,
From a grey and leaden sky,
Covering all the streets and houses,
And the people passing by.
Every flake a different pattern,
Every flake a perfect shape,
Glistening brightly when the sun shines,
Like the icing on a cake.

Snow,
　　Snow,
　　　　Snow,
　　　　　　Snow,
Laughing children playing snowballs,
In the crisp and chilly air.
Rosy cheeks and tingling fingers,
Having fun without a care.
Snowflakes melting, turning slowly,
Into soft and slushy snow,
Icing over when it freezes,
I feel sad to see it go.

The Witch of the South

There was an old witch of the south,
Who had an extremely large mouth.
When she filled it with peas,
And started to sneeze,
They thought it was hailing in Louth.

Air

Swallows dip and swoop and dart,
Across the summer sky,
Using the air to lift their wings,
And carry them up high.

The eagle, soaring with the wind,
Flies far into the sky,
And even the smallest of the birds,
Has to learn to fly.

Balloons will float when full of air,
And kites, when there's a breeze,
All colours and shapes and sizes,
They fly above the trees.

The heaviest plane can stay in the sky,
And the largest ship on the sea,
Can float like the lightest feather.
Now I wonder, why should that be?

Our Bones

Bones in our hips,
And our ankles and our feet.
Bones in our neck,
Where our head and spine meet.
There's a bone in each elbow
Which sometimes feels funny,
And bones in our ribcage,
That is just above our tummy.
Bones in our fingers,
And bones in our toes.
Bones in our arms and legs,
And even in our nose.

Muscles twist and joints bend,
To help us walk and hop.
Without all these bones,
We would simply go, FLOP!

Leaves

Leaves speak.
Can you hear them?

An uncurling and stretching
When blossom is falling.
Leaves waking.

A bustling and rustling
With birds busy nesting.
Leaves shaking.

A soft gentle murmur
In warm sunny weather.
Leaves whispering.

A dripping and drooping
When rain has been
drizzling.
Leaves weeping.

A roaring and rushing
With wind and rain lashing.
Leaves trembling.

A slow shrinking up
When losing their sap.
Leaves sighing.

A crackling and snapping
On cold frosty days.
Leaves falling.

Tickle me Pink

Tickle me pink,
Tickle me pink,
There's a great big spider in the sink.
How did he get there?
I don't know,
But there's no doubt about it,
He'll have to GO!

Castles in the Air

A king lives in a castle,
With walls so thick and tall,
To keep out all his enemies,
When they decide to call.

I haven't got a castle,
Or a drawbridge or a moat,
But in my small front garden,
I'll keep a billy goat.

I'll also have six noisy geese,
Who'll hiss and chase a stranger,
So if you come to my house,
You'll find yourself in danger.

Should you reach the front door,
I'll call out, 'Friend or foe?',
I'll open it to all my friends,
But foes will have to go.

I'd like to have a castle,
And play at being king,
But I can dream, and make pretend,
And be just anything.

The Dinosaur

If I had a dinosaur,
He'd be a special pet.
I don't know what he'd look like,
As I haven't got him yet.
He'd be too big to live indoors
And outside is a problem,
As we've only got a little shed
At the bottom of the garden.
When they find a live one,
I hope they'll think of me,
And not forget, I'd like a pet,
As different as can be.

Swim Dolphin, Swim

Take me away, dear dolphin,
Across a sea of dreams,
To find mystical, beautiful places,
With beaches and forests and streams.
Show me the sun-kissed islands,
Where the palm trees wave in the breeze,
And lizards crawl out of the forests,
And pawpaws grow on trees.
Let us watch the baby turtles,
As they scuttle down to the sea,
Where the glittering waters sparkle,
And the wavelets splash around me.
Let us peep into caves of coral,
Where the angel fish dart and play,
And anemones blossom like opening flowers,
Before we swim on our way.

The Halloween Feast

A witch in the east, made a Halloween feast,
In her rusty, dirty old cauldron.
She mixed slimy brown toads with minced elephant's nose,
And added some ants and her old football pants,
Which she put in to thicken the stew.
The smell was appalling, disgusting, revolting,
And her friends in the Smelly Witch Coven,
Threw their hats in the air, and then pulled up a chair,
As the cauldron was brought from the oven.

Chinese Dragon Dance

Moving along with many feet,
The dragon dances up the street.
Humping his back and shaking his head,
Opening his mouth, with tongue of red.
Moving forwards, writhing, turning.
Enormous eyes, gleaming, burning.
As the rhythm drives him on,
Until the dragon dance is done.

The Frog

Lurking under the lily pads,
Poking his head between the reeds,
Keeping so still, you'd never believe,
A frog was there,
In the water weeds.

Sitting on a sun-warmed stone,
Watching with his bulging eyes,
Patiently waiting for hovering flies,
Still as a statue,
Sits the frog.

Touch him gently and he's gone,
Leaping into murky ponds,
Swimming under feathery fronds,
Hiding underneath the mud,
Lies the frog.

Raising his head above the water,
Surfacing into silvery light,
Can you hear him? That's the frog,
Croak, croak, croaking,
Through the night.

The Fossil

Little pebble on the sand,
Fitting neatly in my hand,
Round and yellow, smooth as cream,
Like a star with dots between.
Hard and solid, like a stone,
While the centre forms a dome.

Little pebble on the sand,
Fitting snugly in my hand,
Were you there long years before,
When dinosaurs walked along this shore?

The Green Man

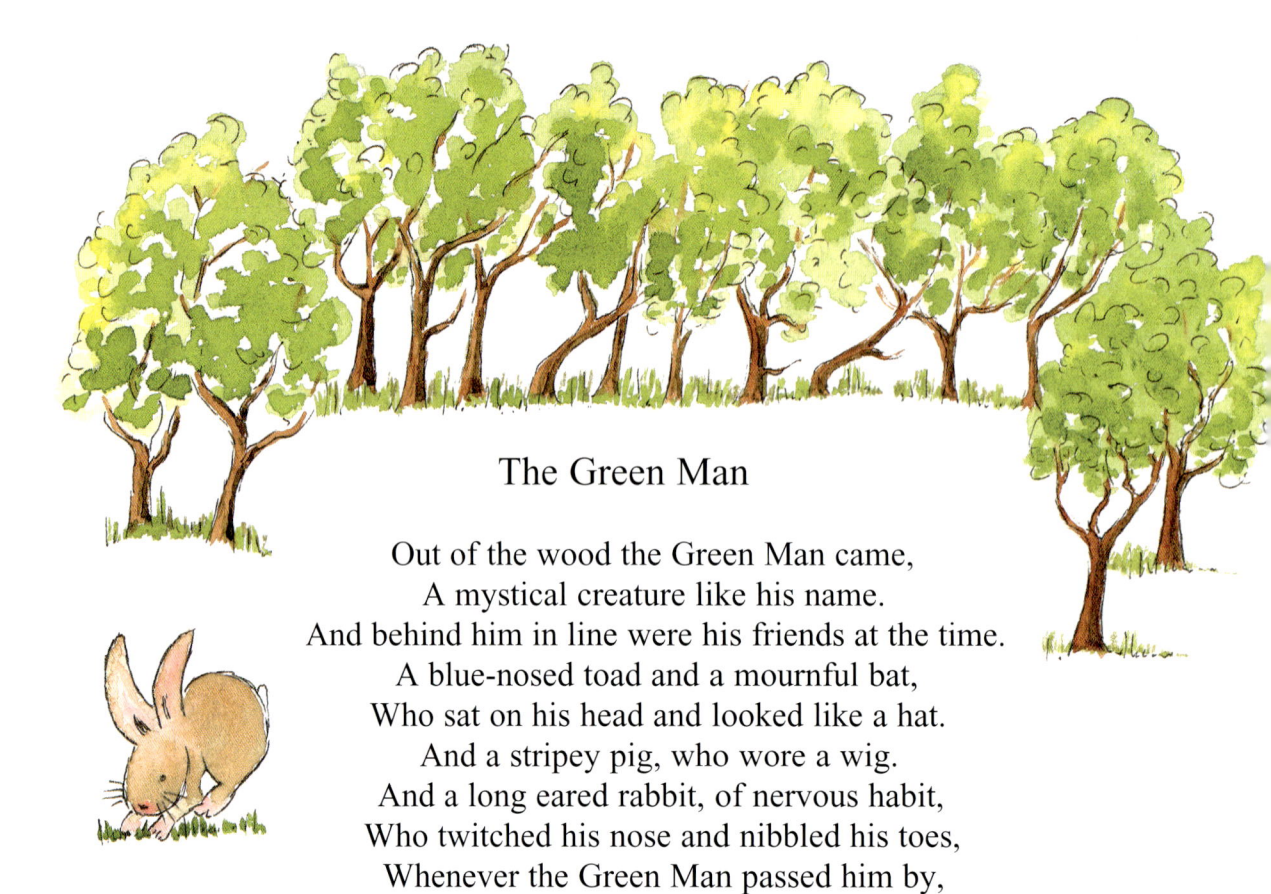

Out of the wood the Green Man came,
A mystical creature like his name.
And behind him in line were his friends at the time.
A blue-nosed toad and a mournful bat,
Who sat on his head and looked like a hat.
And a stripey pig, who wore a wig.
And a long eared rabbit, of nervous habit,
Who twitched his nose and nibbled his toes,
Whenever the Green Man passed him by,
Humming a tune as he looked at the sky.

This was the night when the moon up high,
Shone down on the Green Man's humble pie.
The grasshoppers fiddled and leapt and twiddled,
And the company danced, and twirled and pranced,
In a moonlit glade, where a picnic was laid.
Exhausted with prancing and weary with dancing,
They collapsed in a heap, all ready for sleep.
Then the Green Man rose on his hairy feet,
And exhorted his friends to get up and eat.
When nothing was left they returned in a line,
To party again, at full moon time.

A Long Time Ago

From early morning the streets of town,
Rang to the cries of the sellers of wares.
Down the alleys and round the houses,
Over the cobbles, across the squares.
Carrying baskets, heavily laden,
To tempt the housewife, the master, the maiden,
Shouting and calling, both low and high,
'Come buy, all you people!'
'Come buy! Come buy!'

Lavender! Blue lavender,
To keep your linen sweet.
Take a bunch fair ladies,
As I pass down your street.

Heather! Lucky heather!
White and purple, picked today.
Buy a sprig for your lady love,
And luck will come her way.

Pegs! Pegs! Clothes pegs!
To keep your washing blowing.
Look kindly on the gipsy girl,
And cross her palm with a shilling.

Milk-o! Milk-o!
Creamy white and soft as silk.
Bring your jugs and fill them up,
With a half, a quart, and a pint of milk.

Rags and bones! Rags and bones!
Good prices I will offer.
Show me all you can spare today,
And put money in my coffer.

Pies! Pies! Meat pies!
There are plenty on my tray.
Still warm from the oven,
If you eat them right away.

Amelia, Cordelia, Lucinda Blott

Liked to eat and ate a lot
Of sweets and crisps and sticky things
Like jammy buns and doughnut rings.
Chocolate bars and ice cream cake,
Piles of chips and sausage bake.
Even in her dreams she munches,
Mars Bars, biscuits, Smarties, Crunchies.

Amelia, Cordelia, Lucinda Blott,
Looks just like a fat round pot.
Soon she won't get through the door,
She'll have to sleep upon the floor.
Amelia, Cordelia, Lucinda Blott,
There is no doubt that you must *stop!*
For if you don't — !
You'll go off **POP**!!

Gulp!

My Dad bought a packet of seeds,
To plant in our window box.
'When summer comes,' said my Dad,
'We'll have pink and purple phlox.'
He gave me a seed that was over,
That was nothing like his little lot.
'There you are, son,' he said.
'You can plant that in a pot.'

I watered it, cared for it, watched it,
Until it began to grow,
And was up to the top of the window,
Before Dad's seeds started to show.
Every day it grew taller and taller,
Like a giant amongst his plants.
And people came daily to see it,
Mothers and children and aunts.

Its leaves grew large and hairy,
And its stem was as thick as my arm.
'It's a weed,' said my Dad,
'It needs cutting down.'
'No, Dad, please,' I begged him,
'It's not doing you any harm.'
So it stayed and a green bud appeared
And grew into a large flower head.

I woke one morning and found,
Its petals had opened and spread.
Its shape was like a trumpet,
With lips all spotted with red.
And it bent towards the window,
Where my Dad was sleeping in bed.
Dad woke with a start and looked out,
But before he could speak my plant had him,
And he slid down its throat with a shout.

That was the only meal it had.
But I'm sorry to say,
It was too late for Dad.